Vocabulary for CEM 11+

Welcome to Magical Minds Learning's 11+ Vocabulary book.
This book has exercises to improve your vocabulary for the 11+. Please answer the questions with a circle around the letter like so:

Example	A	B	C	D	E
sad	mean	pretty	upset	scary	happy

Don't worry if you don't know what a word means, the whole point of this book is for you to learn new words and vocabulary!
With words you don't know, it may be helpful to make flashcards or ask somebody to test you on them.
Writing them down helps you remember them better.
Good luck and happy vocabulary learning!

P.S :
Synonyms are words *similar* in meaning,
Whilst *antonyms* are words *opposite* in meaning

Test 1: Synonyms

Select the word closest in meaning to the word in bold.

1

A	B	C	D	E
sad	pretty	upsetting	scary	cheerful

sanguine

2

A	B	C	D	E
shortage	sad	land	thought	plenty

dearth

3

A	B	C	D	E
contest	help	force	disregard	help

compel

4

A	B	C	D	E
angry	helpful	talkative	rich	solemn

earnest

5

A	B	C	D	E
bowl	uproar	thought	provide	quiet

din

6

A	B	C	D	E
lazy	rude	funny	thoughtful	fast

indolent

7

A	B	C	D	E
write	free	help	understand	think

apprehend

8

A	B	C	D	E
feather	cute	calm	thoughtful	attempt

tranquil

9

A	B	C	D	E
leave	help	run	nurture	understand

abandon

10

A	B	C	D	E
colleague	friend	helper	teacher	opponent

adversary

Test 2: Synonyms

Select the word closest in meaning to the word in bold.

1

	A	B	C	D	E
irate	flower	angry	sad	grumpy	enemy

2

	A	B	C	D	E
amiable	kind	friend	angry	scold	comprehend

3

	A	B	C	D	E
insolent	upset	lazy	funny	rude	subtle

4

	A	B	C	D	E
cease	anger	begin	stop	thin	continue

5

	A	B	C	D	E
quaint	curious	sly	sad	fun	strange

6

	A	B	C	D	E
portly	kind	fat	harbour	smart	rude

7

	A	B	C	D	E
attire	fancy	sit	walk	help	clothing

8

	A	B	C	D	E
cumbersome	awkward	fun	sad	fast	sorrow

9

	A	B	C	D	E
melancholy	scary	sorrowful	quiet	dumb	regard

10

	A	B	C	D	E
anecdote	cure	thought	story	item	message

Test 3: Synonyms

Select the word closest in meaning to the word in bold.

1

	A	B	C	D	E
taut	tight	learn	teach	boring	loose

2

	A	B	C	D	E
dubious	angry	loud	shy	scary	doubtful

3

	A	B	C	D	E
bashful	temper	shy	loud	fortunate	upset

4

	A	B	C	D	E
animosity	sure	help	boast	hatred	dream

5

	A	B	C	D	E
deluge	flood	overcome	hypnotise	secret	scare

6

	A	B	C	D	E
seldom	devise	rarely	sell	often	excuse

7

	A	B	C	D	E
feeble	frightened	shy	frail	strong	quick

8

	A	B	C	D	E
purloin	steal	encourage	burn	conquer	eat

9

	A	B	C	D	E
elude	point	core	deter	fall	escape

10

	A	B	C	D	E
apparition	scary	ghost	tremble	view	height

Test 4: Synonyms
Select the word closest in meaning to the word in bold.

1

A	B	C	D	E
cold	definition	difference	number	part

polarity

2

A	B	C	D	E
thought	disaster	funny	impertinent	attempt

impudent

3

A	B	C	D	E
trick	anger	fame	protection	poor

destitute

4

A	B	C	D	E
collect	scatter	choose	collection	move

disperse

5

A	B	C	D	E
clever	dangerous	detected	safe	protect

innocuous

6

A	B	C	D	E
wise	stupid	old	miserable	unhelpful

shrewd

7

A	B	C	D	E
boring	late	punctual	exciting	slow

tardy

8

A	B	C	D	E
fast	courage	fearless	fearful	cowardly

intrepid

9

A	B	C	D	E
hideaway	history	honesty	hobby	match

pastime

10

A	B	C	D	E
saunter	run	hike	jump	march

amble

Test 5: Synonyms

Select the word closest in meaning to the word in bold.

1

	A	B	C	D	E
bazaar	ugly	deal	strange	sell	market

2

	A	B	C	D	E
capacious	capacity	spacious	volume	area	little

3

	A	B	C	D	E
fable	moral	boring	animals	story	unhelpful

4

	A	B	C	D	E
meagre	greedy	stubborn	old	paltry	sufficient

5

	A	B	C	D	E
rogue	scoundrel	child	naughty	ugly	disgusting

6

	A	B	C	D	E
idle	worship	lazy	model	boring	little

7

	A	B	C	D	E
wholly	partly	silly	fully	extra	superfluous

8

	A	B	C	D	E
tenant	careful	person	landlord	owner	occupant

9

	A	B	C	D	E
sober	serious	drunk	thoughtful	miserable	kind

10

	A	B	C	D	E
loathe	slow	detest	bread	adore	disgusting

Test 6: Synonyms
Select the word closest in meaning to the word in bold.

1

A	B	C	D	E
hot	horrid	old	warm	serene

torrid

2

A	B	C	D	E
wise	stupid	weird	variable	unhelpful

fickle

3

A	B	C	D	E
fruitless	plentiful	happy	delicious	tasty

bountiful

4

A	B	C	D	E
ally	hateful	monotony	foe	friend

antagonist

5

A	B	C	D	E
modesty	embarrassed	afraid	miserable	hatred

humility

6

A	B	C	D	E
burn	fire	wood	hot	flag

conflagration

7

A	B	C	D	E
vague	ambiguous	hurt	ailment	flawless

malady

8

A	B	C	D	E
break	fix	hurt	anger	total

aggregate

9

A	B	C	D	E
sea	boat	mystic	above	underground

subterranean

10

A	B	C	D	E
amalgamate	turn	obtain	spin	hallucinate

procure

Test 7: Synonyms

Select the word closest in meaning to the word in bold.

1

A	B	C	D	E
television	isolated	hills	shy	tired

remote

2

A	B	C	D	E
reprimand	disappear	think	tell	bound

admonish

3

A	B	C	D	E
fat	tough	grumpy	muscly	annoy

surly

4

A	B	C	D	E
serious	jewel	believe	temper	charm

talisman

5

A	B	C	D	E
planet-like	moody	happy	kind	cheerful

mercurial

6

A	B	C	D	E
soothe	spin	dizzy	shy	rude

placate

7

A	B	C	D	E
quiet	dumb	audio	volume	sad

mute

8

A	B	C	D	E
first	product	revolve	obtain	mock

deride

9

A	B	C	D	E
kill	scary	poisonous	poison	sneaky

venomous

10

A	B	C	D	E
row	section	line	layer	column

tier

Test 8: Antonyms

Select the word most opposite in meaning to the word in bold.

1

A	B	C	D	E
foe	ally	nemesis	colleague	sister	peace

2

A	B	C	D	E
tranquil	calm	cool	tiring	agitated	fast

3

A	B	C	D	E
vacant	free	occupied	half	great	sneaky

4

A	B	C	D	E
conceal	camouflage	mix	hide	reveal	peek

5

A	B	C	D	E
abandon	start	finish	leave	continue	carry

6

A	B	C	D	E
impudent	respected	respectful	fearful	fearless	secretive

7

A	B	C	D	E
commence	initiate	mid	terminate	amongst	between

8

A	B	C	D	E
slack	learned	taut	knotted	slow	active

9

A	B	C	D	E
shiny	mat	dull	glow	radiant	bored

10

A	B	C	D	E
content	weird	scary	funny	dismal	sneaky

Test 9: Antonyms
Fill in the missing letters so that the new word means the opposite to the word in bold.

1   **common**   un_ _ _ e _

2   **ebb**   f_o_

3   **punctual**   t_rd_

4   **calm**   t_rb_l_n_

5   **occupied**   v_c_n_

6   **generous**   st_n_y

7   **foe**   a_ _ y

8   **continue**   pa_s_

9   **plentiful**   s_an_y

10   **intrepid**   t_m_d

Test 10: Antonyms

Fill in the missing letters so that the new word means the opposite to the word in bold.

1 robust   f_a_ _

2 malady   w_ _ l

3 confident   m_ _ k

4 perplexed   a_ _ u_ed

5 latter   fo_m_ _

6 volatile   st_b_e

7 bogus   g_nu_n_

8 mysterious   u_su_l

9 cantankerous   _ffa_le

10 belligerent   a_i_bl_

Test 11: Synonyms
Select the word closest in meaning to the word in bold.

1

A	B	C	D	E
austere				
money	funny	stupid	harsh	victim

2

A	B	C	D	E
denounce				
whisper	condemn	shame	shout	mad

3

A	B	C	D	E
vanquish				
conquer	disappear	fall	appear	surprise

4

A	B	C	D	E
debris				
beach	sea	rubbish	conserve	converse

5

A	B	C	D	E
tempest				
thief	agreement	run	stomp	storm

6

A	B	C	D	E
periphery				
edge	magic	illusion	centre	soil

7

A	B	C	D	E
hub				
seed	computer	device	core	place

8

A	B	C	D	E
putrid				
thief	health	rancid	harsh	fruit

9

A	B	C	D	E
incredulous				
unbelieving	credible	noteworthy	unfortunate	known

10

A	B	C	D	E
innocuous				
clever	dangerous	detected	safe	protect

Test 12: Antonyms

Select the word closest in meaning to the word in bold.

	A	B	C	D	E
1					
pensive	rapt	jaded	wistful	menacing	thoughtless
2	A	B	C	D	E
lean	chaotic	insignificant	fat	naive	nonchalant
3	A	B	C	D	E
withdraw	celebrate	legit	major	lengthy	advance
4	A	B	C	D	E
minute	atomic	considerable	utter	conduct	engage
5	A	B	C	D	E
tempest	thief	agreement	run	tranquil	storm
6	A	B	C	D	E
eloquent	boundary	stirring	mirage	inarticluate	voluble
7	A	B	C	D	E
grand	windy	unadorned	deep	verbose	inflated
8	A	B	C	D	E
turbulent	calm	scanty	educated	ghoul	near
9	A	B	C	D	E
inaudible	unbelieving	postpone	continue	loud	singular
10	A	B	C	D	E
orotund	hollow	resonating	lazy	industrious	grand

Test 13: Synonyms

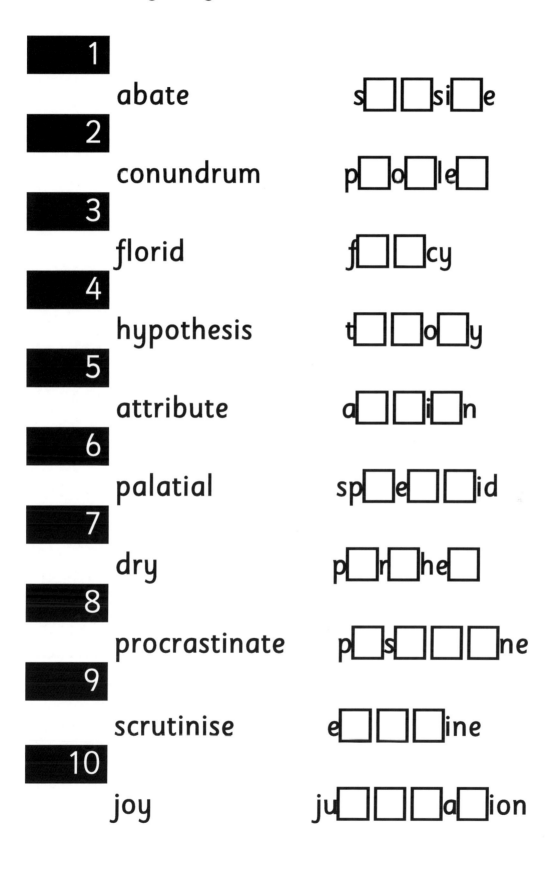

1. abate — s☐☐si☐e

2. conundrum — p☐o☐le☐

3. florid — f☐☐cy

4. hypothesis — t☐☐o☐y

5. attribute — a☐☐i☐n

6. palatial — sp☐e☐☐id

7. dry — p☐r☐he☐

8. procrastinate — p☐s☐☐☐ne

9. scrutinise — e☐☐☐ine

10. joy — ju☐☐☐a☐ion

Test 14: Antonyms

1 barren   □□rtile

2 dour   ch□e□□□l

3 deleterious   h□□□ful

4 new   o□□ol□te

5 repugnant   □leas□□t

6 unlucky   au□p□□□ous

7 inattentive   v□gi□□nt

8 hinder   ad□□□ce

9 overcome   su□□um□

10 take   co□□□□i□u□e

Test 15: Antonyms

1 broad   n ☐ ☐ ☐ o ☐

2 bravery   co ☐ ☐ ☐ di ☐ e

3 cellar   ☐ ☐ ☐ ic

4 gather   ☐ i ☐ t ☐ i ☐ ute

5 tenant   ☐ ☐ ndl ☐ rd

6 idle   ☐ ☐ ☐ ust ☐ io ☐ s

7 merry   m ☐ ☐ t ☐ less

8 wax   ☐ ☐ ne

9 bow   ☐ ☐ ern

10 folly   w ☐ ☐ ☐ om

Answers

Answers are highlighted.

Test 1

1

	A	B	C	D	E
sanquine	sad	pretty	upsetting	scary	**cheerful**

2

	A	B	C	D	E
dearth	**shortage**	sad	land	thought	plenty

3

	A	B	C	D	E
compel	contest	help	**force**	disregard	help

4

	A	B	C	D	E
earnest	angry	helpful	talkative	rich	**solemn**

5

	A	B	C	D	E
din	bowl	**uproar**	thought	provide	quiet

6

	A	B	C	D	E
indolent	**lazy**	rude	funny	thoughtful	fast

7

	A	B	C	D	E
apprehend	write	free	help	**understand**	think

8

	A	B	C	D	E
tranquil	feather	cute	**calm**	thoughtful	attempt

9

	A	B	C	D	E
abandon	**leave**	help	run	nurture	understand

10

	A	B	C	D	E
adversary	colleague	friend	helper	teacher	**opponent**

Test 2

1

A	B	C	D	E
irate | flower | angry | sad | grumpy | enemy

2

A	B	C	D	E
amiable | kind | friend | angry | scold | comprehend

3

A	B	C	D	E
insolent | upset | lazy | funny | rude | subtle

4

A	B	C	D	E
cease | anger | begin | stop | thin | continue

5

A	B	C	D	E
quaint | curious | sly | sad | fun | strange

6

A	B	C	D	E
portly | kind | fat | harbour | smart | rude

7

A	B	C	D	E
attire | fancy | sit | walk | help | clothing

8

A	B	C	D	E
cumbersome | awkward | fun | sad | fast | sorrow

9

A	B	C	D	E
melancholy | scary | sorrowful | quiet | dumb | regard

10

A	B	C	D	E
anecdote | cure | thought | story | item | message

Test 3

	A	B	C	D	E
1					
taut	tight	learn	teach	boring	loose
2	A	B	C	D	E
dubious	angry	loud	shy	scary	doubtful
3	A	B	C	D	E
bashful	temper	shy	loud	fortunate	upset
4	A	B	C	D	E
animosity	sure	help	boast	hatred	dream
5	A	B	C	D	E
deluge	flood	overcome	hypnotise	secret	scare
6	A	B	C	D	E
seldom	devise	rarely	sell	often	excuse
7	A	B	C	D	E
feeble	frightened	shy	frail	strong	quick
8	A	B	C	D	E
purloin	steal	encourage	burn	conquer	eat
9	A	B	C	D	E
elude	point	core	deter	fall	escape
10	A	B	C	D	E
apparition	scary	ghost	tremble	view	height

Test 4

1	A	B	C	D	E
polarity	cold	definition	difference	number	part

2	A	B	C	D	E
impudent	thought	disaster	funny	impertinent	attempt

3	A	B	C	D	E
destitute	trick	anger	fame	protection	poor

4	A	B	C	D	E
disperse	collect	scatter	choose	collection	move

5	A	B	C	D	E
innocuous	clever	dangerous	detected	safe	protect

6	A	B	C	D	E
shrewd	wise	stupid	old	miserable	unhelpful

7	A	B	C	D	E
tardy	boring	late	punctual	exciting	slow

8	A	B	C	D	E
intrepid	fast	courage	fearless	fearful	cowardly

9	A	B	C	D	E
pastime	hideaway	history	honesty	hobby	match

10	A	B	C	D	E
amble	saunter	run	hike	jump	march

Test 5

1 bazaar	A	B	C	D	E
	ugly	deal	strange	sell	**market**

2 capacious	A	B	C	D	E
	capacity	**spacious**	volume	area	little

3 fable	A	B	C	D	E
	moral	boring	animals	**story**	unhelpful

4 meagre	A	B	C	D	E
	greedy	stubborn	old	**paltry**	sufficient

5 rogue	A	B	C	D	E
	scoundrel	child	naughty	ugly	disgusting

6 idle	A	B	C	D	E
	worship	**lazy**	model	boring	little

7 wholly	A	B	C	D	E
	partly	silly	**fully**	extra	superfluous

8 tenant	A	B	C	D	E
	careful	person	landlord	owner	**occupant**

9 sober	A	B	C	D	E
	serious	drunk	thoughtful	miserable	kind

10 loathe	A	B	C	D	E
	slow	**detest**	bread	adore	disgusting

Test 6

1

A	B	C	D	E
torrid	hot	horrid	old	warm	serene

2

A	B	C	D	E
fickle	wise	stupid	weird	variable	unhelpful

3

A	B	C	D	E
bountiful	fruitless	plentiful	happy	scrumptious	tasty

4

A	B	C	D	E
antagonist	ally	hateful	monotony	foe	friend

5

A	B	C	D	E
humility	modesty	embarrassed	afraid	miserable	hatred

6

A	B	C	D	E
conflagration	burn	fire	wood	hot	flag

7

A	B	C	D	E
malady	vague	ambiguous	hurt	ailment	flawless

8

A	B	C	D	E
aggregate	break	fix	hurt	anger	total

9

A	B	C	D	E
subterranean	sea	boat	mystic	above	underground

10

A	B	C	D	E
procure	amalgamate	turn	obtain	spin	hallucinate

Test 7

	A	B	C	D	E
1					
remote	television	isolated	hills	shy	tired
2	A	B	C	D	E
admonish	reprimand	disappear	think	tell	bound
3	A	B	C	D	E
surly	fat	tough	grumpy	muscly	annoy
4	A	B	C	D	E
talisman	serious	jewel	believe	temper	charm
5	A	B	C	D	E
mercurial	planet-like	moody	happy	kind	cheerful
6	A	B	C	D	E
placate	soothe	spin	dizzy	shy	rude
7	A	B	C	D	E
mute	quiet	dumb	audio	volume	sad
8	A	B	C	D	E
deride	first	product	revolve	obtain	mock
9	A	B	C	D	E
venomous	kill	scary	poisonous	poison	sneaky
10	A	B	C	D	E
tier	row	section	line	layer	column

Test 8
Antonyms

1

A	B	C	D	E
A	B	C	D	E

foe — ally | nemesis | colleague | sister | peace

2

A	B	C	D	E

tranquil — calm | cool | tiring | agitated | fast

3

A	B	C	D	E

vacant — free | occupied | half | great | sneaky

4

A	B	C	D	E

conceal — camouflage | mix | hide | reveal | peek

5

A	B	C	D	E

abandon — start | finish | leave | continue | carry

6

A	B	C	D	E

impudent — respected | respectful | fearful | fearless | secretive

7

A	B	C	D	E

commence — initiate | mid | terminate | amongst | between

8

A	B	C	D	E

slack — learned | taut | knotted | slow | active

9

A	B	C	D	E

shiny — mat | dull | glow | radiant | bored

10

A	B	C	D	E

content — weird | scary | funny | dismal | sneaky

Test 9
Antonyms

1 common — unique

2 ebb — flow

3 punctual — tardy

4 calm — turbulent

5 occupied — vacant

6 generous — stingy

7 foe — ally

8 continue — pause

9 plentiful — scanty

10 intrepid — timid

Test 10
Antonyms

1   robust | frail |

2   malady | well |

3   confident | meek |

4   perplexed | assured |

5   latter | former |

6   volatile | stable |

7   bogus | genuine |

8   mysterious | usual |

9   cantankerous | affable |

10   belligerent | amiable |

Test 11
Synonyms

1

	A	B	C	D	E
austere	money	funny	stupid	**harsh**	victim

2

	A	B	C	D	E
denounce	whisper	**condemn**	shame	shout	mad

3

	A	B	C	D	E
vanquish	**conquer**	disappear	fall	appear	surprise

4

	A	B	C	D	E
debris	beach	sea	**rubbish**	conserve	converse

5

	A	B	C	D	E
tempest	thief	agreement	run	stomp	**storm**

6

	A	B	C	D	E
periphery	**edge**	magic	illusion	centre	soil

7

	A	B	C	D	E
hub	seed	computer	device	**core**	place

8

	A	B	C	D	E
putrid	thief	health	**rancid**	harsh	fruit

9

	A	B	C	D	E
incredulous	**unbelieving**	credible	noteworthy	unfortunate	known

10

	A	B	C	D	E
robust	machine	metal	muscle	mechanical	**strong**

Test 12
Antonyms

	A	B	C	D	E
1	A	B	C	D	E
pensive	rapt	jaded	wistful	menacing	thoughtless
2	A	B	C	D	E
lean	chaotic	insignificant	fat	naive	nonchalant
3	A	B	C	D	E
withdraw	celebrate	legit	major	lengthy	advance
4	A	B	C	D	E
minute	atomic	considerable	utter	conduct	engage
5	A	B	C	D	E
tempest	thief	agreement	run	tranquil	storm
6	A	B	C	D	E
eloquent	boundary	stirring	mirage	intarticulate	voluble
7	A	B	C	D	E
grand	windy	unadorned	deep	verbose	inflated
8	A	B	C	D	E
turbulent	calm	scanty	educated	ghoul	near
9	A	B	C	D	E
inaudible	unbelieving	postpone	continue	loud	singular
10	A	B	C	D	E
orotund	hollow	resonating	lazy	industrious	grand

Test 13: Synonyms

1

abate   subside

2

conundrum   problem

3

florid   fancy

4

hypothesis   theory

5

attribute   assign

6

palatial   splendid

7

dry   parched

8

procrastinate   postpone

9

scrutinise   examine

10

joy   jubilation

Test 14: Antonyms

1

barren   fertile

2

dour   cheerful

3

deleterious   helpful

4

new   obsolete

5

repugnant   pleasant

6

unlucky   auspicious

7

inattentive   vigilant

8

hinder   advance

9

overcome   succumb

10

take   contribute

Test 15: Antonyms

1

broad   narrow

2

bravery   cowardice

3

cellar   attic

4

gather   distribute

5

tenant   landlord

6

idle   industrious

7

merry   mirthless

8

wax   wane

9

bow   stern

10

folly   wisdom